TESTIMONIALS

"From the first meeting, I was convinced your program was a fit with an emphasis on: Bold vision, Bold behavior...and...the focus on process....I love the results we are getting including the upbeat 'do or die' spirit, the changed behavior and opening new accounts."

Dean Egan, VP Sales at Roosevelt Paper,
a paper converter and distributor
Video testimonial: https://youtu.be/Ky9whv5voYc

"Andy understands the mindset of an entrepreneur.... He knows how to sell, he knows how to teach people to sell. Andy embraces urgency and 'do or die'; when you have the two you get things done.....He lifted our game...we went from 5 bids to 15 bids."

Robert Koenig, CEO of
Woodbridge International, an M&A firm
Video testimonial: https://youtu.be/qAmCgoUy9G0

"Andy's approach to consulting and training was different than anything I had seen before…We had our best year in 6 years… We got a new level of accountability…Don't delay, get started, I waited too long.

> **Jim Polley,** CEO of Vanguard Dealer Services – they sell
> warranties and insurance products to car dealers
> Video testimonial: https://youtu.be/fUlaNQqpF-U

"The proof of the budding is in the tasting - you have to look at the results. In the last 3 years, we were up 50% year over year in sales, each year…If you aren't working with Andy, you're bleeding to death."

> **Marc Parette,** Co-founder of Parette Somjen Architects,
> Video testimonial: https://youtu.be/xDO7r-adE18

"You really connected with our team, teaching relevant theory and giving example after example of "real stuff", practical examples which were meaningful to our team. The examples were not only compelling -they showed our sales team the universality of what you do…..You get it quickly, you act quickly - you are an entrepreneur"

> **Debbie Tripod,** CEO and owner of Englert Inc.,
> manufactures roofs and gutters:
> Video testimonial by Rob Lowe: https://youtu.be/OOwSRvfgeHc

INNOVATE NOW

SCALE UP WITH 16 BREAKTHROUGH SALES TECHNIQUES

ANDY GOLE

M⊙tivational PRESS®
LEADERS IN GLOBAL PUBLISHING

Published by Motivational Press, Inc.
1777 Aurora Road
Melbourne, Florida, 32935
www.MotivationalPress.com

ISBN: 978-1-62865-645-9

CONTENTS

Foreword...7

Introduction.......................................9

Chapter 1
Overview of the book........................... 14

Chapter 2
Embrace Do or Die vs. Best Efforts 22

Chapter 3
Why bother: Recessions and Why Selling
Had to Change in the Last 60 years................. 30

Chapter 4
Overcome Self-limiting assumptions............... 40

Chapter 5
Create Selling Tools – What's in Your WOW toolbox? . 50

Chapter 6
Change the structure 59

Chapter 7
Learning vs. fixed mindset 67

Chapter 8
Special Techniques: The Impossible Customer,
The 3 Pipe Problem 75

Chapter 9
Bold vision, Bold Behavior 79

Chapter 10

   Innovating to Scale - Using What We Have 92

Chapter 11

   The Pre-mortem For Confirmation Bias 101

Chapter 12

   The Payment in Kind Method (PIK's) 106

Chapter 13

   Risk Aversion 111

Chapter 14

   Do Root Cause Analysis and the

   Standard Sales Call 115

Chapter 15

   How Do You Improve a Sales Organization

   Continuously? 123

Chapter 16

   The Yin and Yang of Selling - a Pause Before

   Emotional Intoxication 127

Chapter 17

   A Path to Emotional intoxication and Innovation -

   a 2 Way Street 133

Chapter 18

   When You Hear "Houston we have a problem" – the

   Apollo 13 Approach, Creating Your Own Solutions . . 142

Chapter 19

   Summing Up 155

   Bibliography. 157

   About the Author - Andy Gole. 160

FOREWORD

In modern culture, it's an oxymoronic idea - selling for emotional intoxication! Consider the direct and indirect impact of negative stereotypes like Willy Loman in **Death of a Salesman;** on the surface "joyous selling" is absurd.

What an extraordinary idea! To potentially achieve emotional intoxication through selling, that is: heroic selling. To take a profession often disparaged and transform it into something sublime.

What makes business development heroic is opening the closed mind, bringing the prospect who says "I'm good" to explore new ideas. This is why salespeople are heroes.

A salesperson on a crusade to help clients, prospects and the company generates self-respect. A powerful selling system, which causes a prospect to behave reasonably - to do behaviors which shows seriousness - garners <u>self-respect</u> for the salesperson.

When salespeople receive respect and self-respect from their work, they are motivated for life.

This book shares 16 ideas for transformative heroic selling - en route to emotional intoxication.

INTRODUCTION

"Get out the 'B' List of Joe's ideas, the ones we didn't implement; let's look at the 3rd idea."

It was the monthly operations meeting. All the department heads were there, except for the safety department, which was handling an emergency.

Joe was flabbergasted. He had joined the company 6 months ago. As a department head, he regularly presented new ideas to top management. Some they implemented, some they didn't. He had a good batting average and was satisfied.

But he had no idea top management was collecting good ideas, which couldn't be implemented at once. There were 30 ideas on that page. It was a WOW moment.

The CEO explained, "Joe, we consider the team's ideas one of our greatest resources. Unfortunately, we can't implement all the ideas at once. Sometimes, there are budget issues, other times, personnel issues and still other times; the idea entails too much risk for the present. So, we inventory the ideas, until the time is right. Today, the time is right for that 3rd idea."

Joe was now super motivated to continue and increase the rate of his idea flow.

Do you have a "B" list of ideas from team members, ideas you can't implement at once? Shouldn't you?

I will share wisdom with you, some of which may be life altering; to benefit, you need to be able to focus.

I said these words to a CEO, who invited me to visit to see if I could help; when I sat down to talk with him, he started answering emails.

You will need some quiet time and some focus to benefit from this book. If you are facing a personal or business emergency that's distracting you, it might not be the best time to read on.

(On the other hand, if the emergency requires new ideas, maybe it is the ideal time to read on.)

Luck can swamp the impact of your ingenuity-based innovation, experience-based wisdom, long study and "do or die" commitment. These elements certainly help make us lucky. But there is no replacement for being at the right place at the right time.

Since we can't control raw luck, we focus on elements susceptible to our control - what we can do to be luckier.

This book offers sixteen practical ideas to be more innovative in sales and thereby luckier.

To be more innovative probably will require change. Here's a way to think about change:

How much change do you want?

Are you willing to pay the price?

Can you change 15% a year?

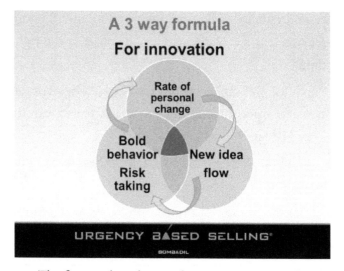

The focus is largely on sales innovation, as sales are a field crying out for innovation. Why?

First, new business development - particularly when competing against entrenched competition - is fraught with uncertainty. The sales process is often stopped before it begins with the "I'm good" objection. We need innovative approaches to break through prospect resistance.

Second, rigorous sales processes - pursued for their own sake - can stifle innovation. Ideally, a rigorous sales process frees the mind to focus on new ideas - as following the selling system takes care of the basics.

When the selling system is a substitute for innovative thinking, entropy sets in with predictable failure.

The basic ideas contained herein generalize to all realms in life. They help make your interactions more effective.

The entire book, taken as a whole, is one path for achieving emotional intoxication - outlined in Chapter 16 - and how emotional intoxication can drive innovation.

Therefore, while each chapter stands by itself, together the whole is vastly greater than the sum of its parts - think 10X+.

If you want to jump in, turn to Chapter 2. Most chapter have links to short videos you will find useful.

For a roadmap, continue reading.

CHAPTER 1
OVERVIEW OF THE BOOK

For an overview, here are the 16 ideas we will meet:

1. **Embrace Do or Die vs. Best Efforts -
   http://bit.ly/BestEfforts**

   Mom and Dad taught us as teenagers: do your best, if you give it your best effort, we're satisfied. What we learn in business is: when facing great uncertainty, when competing against entrenched competition, best efforts should fail 100% of the time. What we need is a "do or die" ethos. Some of us are innovatively lucky - we are confronted with a "do or die" scenario. For the rest of us, our challenge is to evoke the "do or die" mindset without existential threat.

2. **Why bother: Recessions and Why Selling Had to Change in the Last 60 years**

    Why should we worry at all about selling? History suggests a recession will afflict us very soon. Fundamental changes in the world economy necessitate changes in selling.

3. **Overcome Self-Limiting Assumptions -http://bit.ly/self-limiting**

    Up until Bannister ran the 4-minute mile, everyone knew it was impossible. What do you know to be impossible, which may actually be doable? Once, there was a salesperson who was discouraged from calling on a prospect - impossible to close. He drove 400 miles to make a sales call and closed the customer.

4. **Create Selling Tools**

    What's in your WOW toolbox?

    Here are 3 common sales objections: "Your price is too high," "We're good," and "You let us down in the past." How do you use your WOW toolbox to overcome or pre-empt these problems?

5. Change the Structure - http://bit.ly/early-class

All too often, we accept our context as given. With respect to human made rules - particularly social mores - this constrains what we can accomplish. This chapter discusses ways to be thoughtful about changing the structure, changing the ground rules to expand the boundary conditions.

6. Learning vs. Fixed mindset – http://bit.ly/confirm-bias

In her book **Mindset, Carol Dweck distinguishes between two mindsets:**

a) Fixed - which means change, experimentation and, above all, failure is bad.

b) Learning - which means it's our job to learn, to grow, to try new experiences, and it's OK to fail.

This chapter will discuss tactics to enhance your learning mindset.

7. Special Techniques in Innovation

In this chapter we explore the challenge customer and the focused solution, the 3-pipe problem.

8. Bold Vision, Bold Behavior

If you aren't achieving what you want, ask yourself if you are bold enough in your vision and behavior. We will explore social selling (be my friend) vs. business selling (allow me to earn the right to your business).

A related idea is are you being sufficiently unconventional?

George Bernard Shaw wrote:

"The reasonable man adapts himself to the world; the unreasonable one persists in trying to adapt the world to himself. Therefore, all progress depends on the unreasonable man."

9. Innovating to Scale

In his book **Innovating**, author <u>Luis Perez-Breva</u> encourages us to innovate to scale, using the materials, methods and contacts we have. We will explore this idea with respect to sales.

10. The Pre-mortem for confirmation bias, from Tetlock's <u>Superforecasters</u>

<u>http://bit.ly/battleplan1</u>

Professor Tetlock at Wharton has a panel of super forecasters who have substantially above average ability to forecast the future. In his book **<u>Superforecasters</u>**, he describes the methods they use. We will discuss the pre-mortem, a mindset shift in which you assume failure, try to understand why we might fail, then develop a counter strategy.

<u>Luis Perez-Breva</u> suggests a very similar method in his book.

11. The Payment in Kind Method - the Qualifier

When a salesperson returns exuberantly from a sales call and announces: "It was a fantastic call on a new customer, they loved me," was it a slam-dunk or the buyer's con? The payment in kind is a great indicator if it's a real opportunity.

12. Avoid being stopped by risk aversion
http://bit.ly/less-risky

We will discuss **Kahneman's** work on risk aversion in **Thinking Fast and Slow - and** how to profit from it in selling, to make sure we are risk takers. **http://bit.ly/less-risky**

13. Do Root Cause Analysis

http://bit.ly/root-cause1

We will discuss an approach to discover the true causes of problems, to help you improve the quality of your innovating.

14. How do you Improve a Sales Organization Continuously?

What can you do to promote a learning, risk taking sales organization?

15. The Yin and Yang of Selling

How do you balance the hard force in selling (yang) with the soft force (yin)?

16. The Path to Emotional Intoxication

How the heroic mindset is the base of emotional intoxication, both an end and a means to greater creativity.

17. Houston, we have a problem

When the astronauts on Apollo 13 reported "Houston we have a problem", the outlook seemed hopeless. If NASA brought back the 3 astronauts, under impossible conditions, what are you willing to accept as impossible?

With this introduction, I ask, "When is it a good time to begin innovating?"

I hope your answer is NOW!

You are one step closer to emotional intoxication.

CHAPTER 2
EMBRACE DO OR DIE VS. BEST EFFORTS

Video link: http://bit.ly/BestEfforts

We are not seeking novelty or innovation for its own sake, a matter of aesthetic contemplation. We are concerned with practical innovations, which can be implemented, and positively impact the user audience, as well as the innovator's life. Ideally, these innovations will submit to scaling.

Best efforts won't typically roll a big stone up a hill; for this we need a "do or die" commitment. This means committing our energy, our creativity, our heart and soul to a vitally important objective and persisting until the objective is achieved. But we can't take a "do or die" approach to everything, we would be exhausted, we need to prioritize.

Motivation is key to innovation. There may be no better innovation than when facing a real-life "do or die" scenario. For example...

A business owner "looked before he leaped," starting a business selling food packaging, which wasn't viable in the current competitive milieu. The new business had a continuing negative cash flow from the outset. In the 2nd year, the owner both developed a strong "bold vision" for prospects and then found a single "whale" prospect, which could lead to hockey stick growth. Unfortunately, the buyer wasn't interested in the "bold vision," saying, "I'm good, I'm happy with my current supplier of 5 years." Exquisite torture - here was a prospect which would put this businessperson "on the map," yet the prospect wouldn't even talk to him. What would you do in such a scenario? As his last cash reserves were being drained, as he saw himself like George Bailey at the bridge in "It's a Wonderful Life," he asked himself this important question,

"Who is the real decision-maker here? Is it the food packer buying the packaging?"

He decided it was the retailer, who bought the food product from the manufacturer. With his last marketing money, he reached out to 400 food buyers at large retailers, offering a bold vision of what is possible. Here luck entered the picture, as the number 2 US retailer wanted the bold vision and wanted it NOW! (For the full story, please visit this link: bit.ly/bold-vision2).

This was a classic example of necessity being the mother of invention. The necessity provoked a non-conventional action, which was going around the distribution channel. Non-conventional activity can be key to innovation. Are you non-conventional enough?

The businessman described above was lucky - his business was at death's door, which provoked the innovative, non-conventional response.

What if you aren't so fortunate? That is, what if the wolf isn't at your door?

Success can be an obstacle, a great liability to overcome, when considering sales innovation. We often reason with ourselves, Why not let well enough alone?

The law of the marketplace teaches us very few, if any, business or product life cycles are forever. What is more likely is competitor emulation and innovation shorten profitable life cycles. The best time to innovate - and possibly cannibalize your current position - is when we are riding high, when sales and profits are strong. We have the wherewithal to finance innovation, to withstand its setbacks.

Here's a graphic, which might help guide you to the needed mindset for innovation, always seeing yourself at the edge of a cliff.

Always see yourself at the edge of a cliff, being pushed back by a ferocious bear. It's a "do or die" scenario. No matter how strong our current position, we face competitive developments - possibly unseen presently - which could push us to the end of the cliff, including: changes in customer demand, new products - either generic or close substitutes - government regulations, and international factors.

We shouldn't wait for the wolf or bear to appear - bring them into your life, into your mindset to spur practical innovation.

In <u>Journey to Ixthlan</u>, Don Juan teaches Carlos Castaneda to use death as an advisor. Do you?

Think of Mickey's admonition to Rocky (in Rocky III), when he tried to discourage Rocky from fighting Clubber Lang,

"Well, Rock, let's put it this way. Three years ago, you were supernatural. You were hard and nasty. You had this cast iron jaw. But then, the worst thing happened to you that could happen to any fighter. You got civilized."

See: http://bit.ly/rocky_1

Are you too civilized to innovate? Have you forgotten your roots, the "do or die" scenarios you or your business faced en route to success? Rediscover these roots, keep them in focus, to spur your innovation.

It's obvious we need the "do or die" commitment when we are at the edge of the cliff. What is less obvious is we often need the same commitment just to open a new account, when it isn't life or death.

The salesperson's bane - "I'm good" - can stop up to 95% of all selling opportunity. Prospects will say I'm good, even when they are drowning - whether they know it or not. If we accept the prospect's judgement, it's lose/lose/lose.

In order to persevere, we need to be on a 3-way crusade:

1) To build our personal book of business.

2) To build the company's business.

3) To save the prospect - often from making sub-optimal decisions.

To succeed in this quest, we need:

1) Strong self-belief - in ourselves, our company.

2) To care about the prospect, who is making a sub-optimal decision.

3) A focused "do or die" approach to break through the resistance, so that the prospect hears our message.

If you want to succeed at business development, do or die is a way of life.

You are one step closer to emotional intoxication.

CHAPTER 3
WHY BOTHER: RECESSIONS AND WHY SELLING HAD TO CHANGE IN THE LAST 60 YEARS

Embracing "do or die" is a lot of work, as are many ideas in the book. Why bother?

It's about time for another recession - consider the history of recessions since 1980.

Recent recessions

July 1981 – November 1982

July 1990 – March 1991

March 2001- November 2001

December 2007 – June 2009

Almost every 10 years.

When do you expect the next recession? Do you have a plan?

URGENCY BASED SELLING®

BOMBADIL

How are you preparing for the next recession?

One of the best anti-recession strategies is increasing market share now - so when sales shrink in the coming recession, our position is more sustainable. We can hold more of our core resources intact - including essential team members. This probably requires change.

Even if an impending recession wasn't a factor, changes in the selling milieu over the last 60 years necessitate a change in selling.

A. The Customer is Always King – But it has be a win/win

We all know the customer is king, but this principle backfires when we agree to an adversarial buying program that diminishes our selling. For instance: The Purgatory of Call Me Back in 2 Weeks.

We have all had the experience:

1. We meet the prospect, get invited to bid and submit our bid, are told to follow up in 2 weeks.

2. We call back at the agreed upon time to follow up and are told: "I haven't looked at the proposal yet; call me back in 2 weeks."

3. So we call back in 2 weeks, and get told, "Call me back in 2 weeks."

This continues, sometimes indefinitely. I once spent 90 minutes on the phone with a prospect during several calls in a 3-month period, discussing everything but the proposal - which was still on his follow up stack.

This seems to continue forever, at times.

Some people call this…The Purgatory of Call me Back in 2 weeks.

Here's a troubling thought – could our selling system be encouraging this?

B. Safe vs. Serious Conversations

The core of selling is conversations. There are two types:

1) Safe – the prospect will never give you any business; they are in the conversation for

another reason. Typically, they want a 3rd price to gauge the effectiveness of their buying from the incumbent.

2) Serious – the prospect has a compelling need and is willing to discuss it.

How do you know if you're in a serious conversation (assuming it's not a 1 call close)?

See: http://bit.ly/3Fatalflaws

We watch what the prospect does, not what the prospect says. We need PIK's, payments in kind. Thought quesiton: Are we encouraging the prospect to act seriously?

C. Major Post World War II eras in selling

1. Social Selling - Noah's Ark through 1950's

2. Facts and Benefits – 1950's – 1960's

3. Solution Selling – 1960's through 1980's

4. Challenging the customer – the modern era – selling on Urgency!

1. Social Selling - effective post WWII

Social selling is highly effective in a limited competition environment. For example, in the Post WWII era, where the United States had most of the factories in the World.

Companies could compete on:

1) Golf outings

2) Partying

3) Belonging to the right club or social circle

Question: Is this as effective as it once was? If not, why not?

Did social selling encourage appropriate PIK's?

2. Facts and Benefits – 1960's

As competition heats up in 1960's worldwide, sellers have to give prospects actual business reasons to buy; meeting a compelling need.

Consider the introduction of audiocassettes as an alternative to records: cassettes are more convenient, portable.

Facts and benefits are an early selling effort to meet the challenge of increased competition. It is very effective when social selling is the alternative. For instance,

If you need to play music in a remote location, you need audiocassettes. Social relations can't win the day for records.

We discovered choosing between social selling and benefits selling is a false dichotomy. We need both.

Social selling might give prospects a reason to hear our story. Benefits selling gives prospects a reason to buy.

3. Solution Selling: 1960's through 1980's – IBM and Xerox

A further market development involves segmenting markets and offering tailored solutions. This entails a consultative sell. First identify the problem, and then present the benefits we offer to solve the problem.

This both expands the market and provides a "defendable position."

A defendable position is hard to emulate. Classic defendable position strategies include:

Low cost producer, Patents, trademarks, branding

Michael Porter, Harvard Business School Professor, publishes a classic article in 1979 on defendable positions. His 1980 book – <u>Competitive Strategy</u>, follows this. He advocates establishing long-term defendable positions. With long product life cycles, large investments in defendable positions could be justified.

The way we sold made sense for the time.

In the 1960's and even the 1970's, the United States is still the dominant manufacturer in the world.

4. The Modern Era – 1990's on – Hyper competition

In 1990's traditional defendable positions erode, as markets change more rapidly. What drove the change?

1) Rapidly changing technology – e.g. – Internet replaces printed marketing materials

2) Overseas' competition

Two books explore this development:

<u>Hyper competition</u> - Richard D'Aveni

<u>Competing at the Edge</u> - Shona L. Brown, Kathleen M. Eisenhardt:

Long-term defendable positions, appropriate to limited competition, give way to:

The quest for short-term advantage. Key drivers in the U.S. economy:

1. Shorter business life cycles by 1990's

2. Very expensive to constantly innovate

There is a latent demand for a selling system which substitutes for high capital investment in creating defendable space. This requires a change in the selling system, to a method that constantly creates and satisfies needs.

5. Urgency Based Selling Process – for the modern era – making the important urgent, challenging the prospect and evolving as rapidly as needed.

Focusing on urgency challenges the customer. This identifies both existing and potential urgent needs. By taking a stand, this compels the prospect to enter a serious discussion and act respectfully.

Urgency condenses the selling cycle and catalyzes relationship formation. When we start with urgency, it also gives the prospect a reason to form a social relationship.

Urgency selling remedies these problems:

1. Lack of urgency by prospects and sales force.
2. Wasted time in safe situations.
3. Sales force blackmail of owners – particularly in treating prospect and clients as private property (prospect and clients are company property – its top management's job to set the risk level taken by the sales team).

Urgency Based Selling* makes possible exponential sales growth – with limited investment.

In challenging the prospect, we discover where the prospect is "bleeding to death" - which means the prospect has a substantial problem and may not know it - and show how we are the best or only solution (defendable position). This not only covers situations where the prospect knows his/her pain. It also covers situations where the prospect isn't aware they are bleeding to death – the educational, missionary sale.

Proper implementation improves closing ratios to the 50% mark.

D. Conclusion – selling in the modern era

We are in the modern era of shorter product life cycles, and intense competition. We need lower cost alternatives to risky capital investment. We must challenge the customer to earn the right to the sale. Urgency Based Selling˚ does the job.

How about your company?

How are you selling?

You are one step closer to emotional intoxication.

CHAPTER 4
OVERCOME SELF-LIMITING ASSUMPTIONS

A self-limiting assumption takes you out of the game. You can't succeed, because you assume this is so at the outset. Do you have any self-limiting assumptions that prevent innovation?

Think about running the 4-minute mile. Before 1954, the conventional wisdom was, "it's impossible. The human body isn't designed to run a 4-minute mile." Or is it?

Roger Bannister didn't start by assuming the 4-minute mile was impossible. He designed a training program to achieve this milestone. Six weeks later John Landy broke Bannister's record.

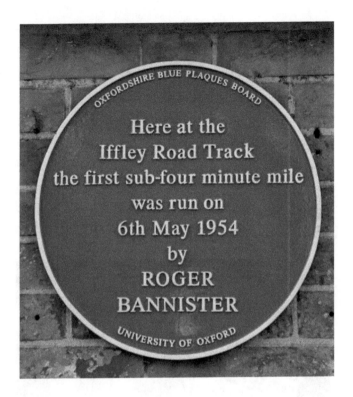

How often do we fail to achieve our sales objectives because of self-limiting assumptions? This was true at a company selling off-spec materials, in business for 80 years, yet not having a single testimonial.

When confronted with the idea of a testimonial project, the 10-, 15- and 20-year veteran salespeople agreed it was impossible, saying, "Our customers don't want to admit they do business with us. They would never write a testimonial." A 24-year-old new hire didn't know it was impossible and was able to obtain a testimonial within two weeks. The veterans were a bit embarrassed and had their first testimonials within one month. Now, they have over 50 written testimonials and a short video testimonial. To read the full story and the power of testimonials for sales innovation, please visit: http://bit.ly/self-limit

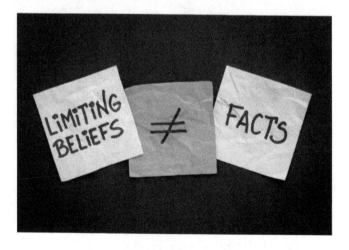

Do you have any self-limiting assumptions, which might cut off your innovation before you begin?

These assumptions might take the form of:

1) We've always done it this way.

2) It can't be done.

3) I'm not taking a chance with my customer.

This latter point stifles innovation in many companies, when the most successful salespeople refuse to test new ideas and products. They "protect" their customers from testing needed innovation. And innovation fails or never gets started.

Here's a strong sales team innovation project: tell the Bannister story, tell a similar experience from the company's history; then, challenge sales team members to write down any potential self-limiting assumptions. Afterwards, discuss the self-limiting assumptions, and go to work on overcoming them.

A rookie salesperson was told to avoid a certain prospect - nobody in the industry could close the prospect. It was a whale in size, but a waste of time. Ignoring common wisdom, the salesperson drove 400 miles to meet and ultimately close this whale.

Another way to discover self-limiting assumptions is to consider the boundary conditions of our knowledge. Identify what you know to be the outer limit - e.g. how often you can call a prospect - then push beyond that limit, by devising a method to "earn the right?"

Could we be on a false summit?

URGENCY BASED SELLING®

Once there was a marketing company selling to pharmaceutical brand managers. Everyone knew you were lucky to get one appointment a year. We started from the belief you could secure another appointment and conceived a legitimate reason for a 2nd appointment. Surprise! We started getting additional appointments.

Then, we added the idea of the "quarterly checkup." More appointments, more selling opportunities.

Accepting prospect guilt as given can be another self-limiting assumption.

Is guilt bottling up sales?

Are you helping the person you are protecting?

URGENCY BASED SELLING®

BOMBADIL

Very often a prospect will be reluctant to switch suppliers out of a sense of loyalty to the current supplier - either to the company or the salesperson. The prospect feels a sense of guilt at "breaking the relationship."

If you accept this emotional response, are you really helping the decision-maker or the organization? They have been making a sub-optimal decision. If you walk away in the face of guilt, you allow the prospect to continue making poor decisions.

Sometimes we need to escalate our activities, reach out to a higher-level decision-maker, to deal with a buyer's sense of guilt. A buyer's sense of guilt at switching suppliers may not align with the owner's objectives. Going higher in an organization can bring the decision into a more objective realm.

Selling is saddled with a series of paradoxes, which can become self-limiting assumptions. For example:

1) **On change** - salespeople know they can't open new customers, unless a prospect is willing to change. Yet, so many salespeople hold themselves above change - change is for others. If sales are off, the problem is elsewhere - with the product, the pricing, the dating terms, anything but the salesperson.

2) **Urgency vs. Neediness**

   A prospect expects us to act with a sense of urgency - we respond to the prospect's needs. Yet, every time we do so, the prospect wonders, "Is this seller needy? Can I get a fire sale?" This is a real problem for salespeople, a problem we resolve in the chapter on PIK's.

3) **The Platypus/dual nature of business developers**

On the one hand, business developers are employees, on the other hand, we need to act entrepreneurially like owners to succeed. Salespeople who don't integrate these two roles are often unhappy. This becomes a self-limiting assumption. A resolution is to align with the company's goals and always act like you would as an owner.

Finally, consider the customer we have let down in the past. They are refusing to buy from us because the "burnt hand remembers the match," and they are loyal to the incumbent vendor. Should we "give up," because the situation is hopeless?

Once a salesperson was facing this "hopeless" scenario, but didn't know the specifics of the past disappointment. He was in his first year on the job; the disappointment took place 10 years earlier. After making cold field calls for 6 months with no success, he finally asked the business owner to discuss the disappointment.

The owner said,

"During the 2007-2009 recession, we fell behind in our payments and you cut off our credit. Your competitor stepped up to the plate and extended our credit line and credit terms. Why the hell should I ever give you any business now that I don't need you?"

WOW. We can easily sympathize with the business owner. However, our job is to reopen the customer. Here's what the salesperson said,

"I am sorry we let you down, and I understand how upset you are. I would be also. I have a question, "Do you believe in second chances in life?"

The business owner said he did believe in second chances.

The salesperson asked, "How can we earn the right to a second chance with you?"

And the conversation was re-opened; the owner was willing to give the salesperson another chance, when the circumstances were right.

Who says you can't sell a prospect you once let down?

What self-limiting assumptions prevent you from innovating?

You are one step closer to emotional intoxication.

CHAPTER 5
CREATE SELLING TOOLS
– WHAT'S IN YOUR WOW
TOOLBOX?

Here are 3 common sales problems:

1. Your price is too high

2. We're good

3. You let us down in the past

The WOW! Tool box can turn red oceans into blue oceans

URGENCY BASED SELLING®

BOMBADIL

Once there was a company so well known amongst customers and prospects, that their largest prospect segment was customers they had let down in the past. The prospects would say, "burn me once, shame on you; burn me twice shame on me." And "the burnt hand remembers the match." The sales team couldn't get any traction with the largest prospect segment.

In sales training, the salespeople reasonably asked the trainer, "How can I handle this objection?"

The trainer responded: "I can't, but you can." How? By getting testimonial letters from customers who "threw us out," then gave us a chance and were glad they did.

The sales team secured about 6 testimonials from such revived customers. These testimonials helped them open other skeptical previous customers.

If we don't address these issues:

1) Your price is too high

2) We're good

3) You let us down in the past

We shouldn't expect any business. What do you have in your Wow toolbox to deal with these issues?

Powerful testimonials can be very helpful. Let's say your toolbox is light on testimonials. Whose job is it to secure objection refuting powerful testimonials?

Salespeople often see this as management's job or perhaps marketing's job. Yet, the salesperson usually has the best personal relationships to make the request.

The best idea is for you to draft the testimonial you want your big fans to write for you.

When should you ask for a testimonial? After they praise you for a job well done is a great time. Explain the importance of dealing with skeptics, and offer to write the testimonial, to make it easier for them.

We like to write the testimonials for two reasons:

1) So they get done – if we wait for the client to write the testimonial, it might take a very long time.

2) So the testimonial says what we want it to say. In the case described above, we wanted the customer to address a very specific issue.

How should you approach getting testimonials? On a "do or die" basis. There really isn't any other practical way to approach life and accomplishments.

Here's a starter kit template for addressing the objections at the beginning of this section:

1) Your price is too high

Salespeople probably report they encounter this objection above all others. (We'll discuss below why "I'm good" is the real deal killer). You need to identify several customers who initially said, "Your price is too high," but eventually gave you a chance and became a loyal customer.

Here's a template you might use for your price is too high.

Dear,

When you first asked for an appointment, I granted one, because you have a well-regarded product in the marketplace. At the same time, I was afraid your pricing would be too high. It was. So, I passed initially. After all, <u>we make money when we buy, not when we sell.</u>

Fortunately, you kept in touch. During one discussion, I mentioned the challenges I had with your competitor, and how I wished I could buy your product at a competitive price. I was finally open to what you had been saying all along; focus on total cost vs. first cost.

Up until that moment, I was focused on first cost, the purchase order price. You helped me do an economic justification, which showed I would save money almost immediately, by paying you more - by focusing on cost in use.

Sounds counterintuitive to pay more, but it's better to do it once right, than many times incorrectly.

If anyone is balking at paying you for your quality product, have him or her call me. I will let them know what's really expensive – poor quality.

2) I'm good

Although the price objection is cited most often, "I'm good" probably shuts down 80-90% of all opportunity. You can't get to the price objection if you aren't even in the game.

Ideally, you will identify several customers who started out by saying "I'm good." We would like to have several letters or videos from clients, conveying the following sentiment.

Dear,

When you called on me, I thought to myself – that's all I need, another carton salesperson. So, I told you "I'm good," believing it to be so.

After all, we have been successful for years, no significant problems with our existing suppliers.

But you were so persistent. You didn't just stay in touch, you continued to share new ideas, trends and market research, which was novel and useful to me. You always added value when we talked or met.

Made me start to wonder why my existing suppliers weren't doing the same.

Finally, your contributions loomed so large; I felt I had to give you a chance. That's when I found out I should have been giving you most of my business all along.

The key lesson you taught me is to be open to new ideas.

We look forward to many years of working together.

3) You let me down

In a very mature market, very often we need to return to customers who stopped buying because we let them down. The same customers who tell us "the burnt hand remembers the match."

You will need to find customers you let down, who stopped buying, then resumed and are now loyal customers. Here's a letter you might adapt.

Dear,

Years ago, your company let me down with a service failure. When you didn't deliver on time, I missed a critical ship date - as a result, I almost lost my major customer; my promises are conditioned on the promises I receive from key vendors.

You subsequently called on me for several years, trying to get back in, but as the saying goes "the burnt hand remembers the match."

Fortunately, you did more than call on me. Your company changed. You revolutionized your workflow to prevent the kind of service failure which caused me to drop you as a supplier.

I didn't start to take you seriously until your plant manager joined you on a call. Then, I visited your plant to see the changes with my own eyes.

I was impressed with what I saw.

With the changes you made, you leapfrogged the methods used by my other suppliers.

I tested you for a 6-month period, liked the results and have now returned you to an 80% share of wallet.

In the end, I have to say I believe in 2nd chances; if someone makes good and it's to our advantage, we will give you the 2nd chance.

Thanks.

Note:

WOWs are two-edged swords. If you don't get any Wows, it probably means your sales presentation isn't strong enough.

If you do get WOWs, you need to harvest customer commitment to action (see chapter on PIK's below).

You are one step closer to emotional intoxication.

CHAPTER 6
CHANGE THE STRUCTURE

video link: http://bit.ly/early-class

Let's say you are registering for your last semester in college, there's a course you have been dying to take for years, it's being offered, but only at 7 am. And you sleep until 10 am. What can you do? Suck it up, take the course? Take the course with a friend attending every other class, with whom you share notes? Ask a friend to record the lecture? Stay up all night, take the 7am class, then go to sleep?

You probably faced this challenge or know someone who did. What to do?

How about asking the university administration to change the time they offer the class - so you can sleep late? Insane, impossible! "Allowing you to sleep late" probably wouldn't be a compelling motivation for the administration. How about, "It will increase class attendance and prevent poor attendance from causing the course to be dropped." This might work! In fact, it did, see the video at this link: http://bit.ly/ early-class

What a gift to have at a young age, knowing almost anything is possible if you strive for it!

Solving a personal problem - like the early college class - is a great way to begin your quest for innovation. This helps you explore if you can change the way "things are done". What personal challenge can spur your innovation?

Ask yourself, What opportunity lies directly in your path, ideally a passion, something you hesitated to embrace because "it's not the way we do things?"

All too often, we accept our context as given. With respect to human made rules - particularly social mores - this constrains what we can accomplish. This chapter discusses ways to be thoughtful about changing the structure, changing the ground rules, to expand the boundary conditions.

The biggest reason salespeople won't challenge the structure is: they want to be liked. They embrace traditional social values - be my friend - to the exclusion of appropriate business values - let me earn the right to your profitable business. Which might require me to challenge you. Social sellers avoid conflict. Social and business values don't present an "either-or" option; it's an "and." When business values are sufficiently diminished, so does closing new customers in the face of entrenched competition. For a 2-minute video on social vs. business values, please click here: http://bit.ly/social-vs-business

Overreliance on social values can preclude innovation, which typically requires us to go outside of the box, embrace conflict, and challenge another person's thinking.

To change the structure in the world around us, we typically need to begin at home, change our thinking regarding relationships.

Are you ready to change the structure around you to achieve your goal? What non-conventional behavior can you embrace to move a sale forward?

A classic structural obstacle for salespeople is not going high enough in the food chain. You don't want to "ruin the relationship" with the decision-maker who allows you to visit. Is there really a relationship to ruin? Not if they aren't buying anything or "not buying enough."

Once there was a salesperson who called on a prospect every 3 weeks for 8 months. The call reports were glowing. "Great meeting toured the plant, no needs. Next time: Great meeting, we went to lunch, no needs. Followed by: Great meeting discussed industry trends, no needs."

The only problem was the salesperson sold a product the prospect could have bought on each meeting, for the 8 months. Finally, with coaching, the salesperson changed the structure and called the prospect's President. The receptionist decided to connect the salesperson to the buyer who angrily said, "You're going over my head! You want to know why I haven't bought from you - your pricing is high; your service and quality are lousy! That's why I don't buy from you!"

WOW. Was this good or bad, to find out how the prospect really viewed the salesperson and his offering? Would you want to know?

A sales trainer once went around the room, asking every salesperson, "With what % of your customers can you pick up the phone and call the President or

CEO?" Here were the answers: 10%, 15%, 20%, 5%, 60%, 20%, 10%, and 5%.

Wow! One salesperson knew 60% of the CEO's. How was this possible? We asked him. Whenever he contacted a new prospect, he started by calling the President. He was usually referred to a buyer, but in the meantime, he set up a communication channel to the CEO.

You can also change the structure by identifying and addressing more self-limiting assumptions. There are 3 Fatal Flaws in selling - are you guilty of any of these?

The 3 Fatal Flaws destroy BD

 Assuming prospect enters conversation with serious intention

Safe vs. serious conversations

 Assuming prospect believes what we say

 Assuming prospect knows how to make a decision

URGENCY BASED SELLING

BOMBADIL

For a video, please go to this link: bit.ly/3Fatalflaws

The first fatal flaw is to assume you are in a serious conversation because the prospect is talking to you. The default position for prospects is a price check. You need to earn the right to a serious conversation, usually by making a bold vision obvious.

The second fatal flaw is thinking the prospect believes what you say. In general, they don't because of skepticism and risk aversion. The chapter on selling tools provides some ideas on how to address this Fatal Flaw.

Finally, it is wrong to assume the prospect knows how to make a good decision. In general, prospects infrequently make vendor switching decisions or big purchase decisions. They are not experts at these decisions and need your help - including a decision-making worksheet.

Make a list of the constraints preventing you from moving forward on a passionately held objective. Are these constraints truly impossible? Now you have a project list - of constraints you need to change.

Cautionary note: There will probably be a fair amount of "windmill tilting" as you strive for the seemingly impossible. Be prepared to fail; failure is a great teacher. We need to be tough enough to absorb the emotional setbacks associated with failure.

You are one step closer to emotional intoxication.

CHAPTER 7
LEARNING VS. FIXED MINDSET

Video Link: http://bit.ly/confirm-bias

A sales team was in the 2nd month of training, when they focused on getting more introductions from big fans. In fact, everyone had an assignment to bring in an introduction the next week. In the one to one coaching, it was Sally's turn to report. Sally was the key account manager on the company's biggest customer, who did about 40% of the volume. Here's how the conversation flowed:

Manager: How did it go? Did you get any introductions?

Sally: No

Manager: Oh, how many people did you ask?

Sally: No one.

Manager: Did you know that everyone had the assignment to bring in one introduction?

Sally: Yes.

Manager: So, what happened?

Sally: You don't understand, since I was hired 22 years ago, it has been my job to wait for the phone to ring. When our clients call us, I race over, find out what they need and make sure they are delighted with our performance and service.

Sounds like Sally has the closed mindset.

In her book **Mindset, Carol Dweck distinguishes between two mindsets:**

1) Fixed - which means change, experimentation and, above all, failure is bad.

2) Learning - which means it's our job to learn, to grow, to try new experiences, and it's OK to fail.

If you are going to be a successful innovator, you need to both internalize learning mindset and persuade important constituents to embrace the same. These constituents might be: prospects, customers, vendors, and your CEO.

What about Sally? Could she be moved from fixed to learning mindset?

Manager: Sally, you are blocking the superhighway. Clients who are our big fans are our greatest selling asset. We are only selling 3 of 50 divisions we can sell at your client. If you don't ask for introductions, no one will. Don't block the superhighway.

P.S. Two weeks later, Sally had an introduction.

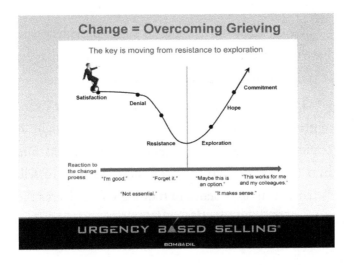

Often, we need to move someone from fixed to learning mindset, coaching people from resistance to exploration on the change curve.

For most of us, change entails overcoming grieving - we grieve over what we gave up.

These ideas are well presented in the book **On Death and Dying.** For effective sales innovation, we typically need to persuade prospects to move from resistance to exploration, from fixed mindset to open mindset.

Here's a story, which involves both changing the structure (from the last chapter) and learning mindset.

We all know buyers like to select providers who have industry relevant experience. So, we might argue, if you don't have relevant experience, why bother?

Twenty-five years ago, a business owner heard a presentation by his accounting firm, thought it could be stronger and suggested the 7 partners hire him (their client) to teach the partners how to sell. What was his experience in training CPA's? Here's the conversation they had:

CPA firm: Have you ever trained CPA's before?

Client: No.

CPA Firm: Do you have any testimonial letters to show your success with other firms?

Client: No.

CPA Firm: Have you ever trained any company at any time?

Client: No.

CPA Firm: Do you have any curriculum to share with us, to give us an idea of what you would teach us?

Client: No.

CPA Firm: Then, what the hell makes you think you can do this?

The client said: I saw you present to me, I know what is possible, and I can help you get much better.

Two CPA partners invited their client to join them on a sales call to observe and learn, perhaps to suggest specific changes the CPAs could implement. His instructions were to zip his lips, say nothing. Afterwards, they would debrief. The client followed the rules for the first hour of the sales call. Then he changed the structure, raised his hand, asked the prospect 2 questions and closed the sale. A month later the CPA firm hired him; during the 6-month training period, the firms' closing ratio went from 20% to 80%.

The Business Newspaper for the Tax and Accounting Community

ACCOUNTINGTODAY

ACCOUNTING TODAY: JUNE 22-JULY 12, 1998

Gikow Bierman & Talesnick teaches clients art of the deal

by John Fuller

ROSELAND, N.J. — Closing the deal. It's a phrase often identified with fast-talking salesmen that strikes fear into the hearts of some accountants.

Gikow, Bierman & Talesnick wanted to overcome their sales anxieties and so developed a sales training program with one of their clients. The program worked so well that they have been selling their expertise for a year-and-a-half at an average of $15,000 per program. The training consists of five classes, field observation and follow up. For their innovative thinking, the Roseland, N.J.-based firm received an Accounting Today Gold Medal Award for Achievement in Client Service.

The firm wanted to improve its sales closing statistics, but nothing seemed to work. The sales gurus would come and go, but their advice was soon forgotten. Firm accountants wanted a customized sales training program, and they discovered the solution was closer than they thought.

A client, Andy Gole, president of AMG Corp., convinced the firm that, although his successful sales record

was as a distributor and wholesaler of toys and novelty items, his sales methods were universal. Gole said that he could provide the training the firm needed.

Gole spent six months working with the partners, going out on sales calls and observing their selling techniques. He developed classroom training and had the accountants role play to deal with a series of customer objections. Gole built his sales technique around teaching sellers to overcome the customers' natural skepticism.

"Salespeople have to know the closing conditions and be in control," Gole said. "You have to earn the right to ask certain questions and have to know when to ask them. We also developed a routine on how to overcome objections."

Gole tailored his sales techniques to the needs of the firm and helped the CPAs become more at

ease with selling.

"Andy saw our sales technique and stayed with us," said partner Burt Bierman. "I think most accountants have a hard time closing, and Andy helped us develop closing questions that we were comfortable with."

Burt Bierman, right, of Gikow, Bierman & Talesnick, and AMG Corp. president Andy Gole know how to make clients sign on the dotted line.

For the full story, click here: http://bit.ly/bold-vision1

<u>Accounting Today</u> published a front-page article discussing how the CPA firm invited the client to become part of their consulting group.

This story is a powerful example of the learning mindset. We normally (perhaps unfairly) associate the accounting profession with resistance to change. The story celebrates the learning mindset, the CPA firm's ability to explore an unexpected possibility.

It also illustrates how a new business can be started, by asking two questions. Can you think of two questions to start a new business?

How do you feel about learning? So much of what we learned in school is obsolete within a few years. One key to success in life and in innovation is being a non-stop learner.

How much do you learn, how much do you change each year?

Imagine if you added 10-15% to your usable knowledge.

How do we move people along the change curve, from resistance to exploration? One innovative method is bold vision, and bold behavior.

You are one step closer to emotional intoxication.

CHAPTER 8
SPECIAL TECHNIQUES: THE IMPOSSIBLE CUSTOMER, THE 3 PIPE PROBLEM

A great way to develop new sales ideas is to focus on the "customer you are never going to sell" and develop a plan to sell them.

Sounds crazy, right? Time is precious, we are so busy, we are meant to prioritize, and focus on meaningful pipeline opportunity. Why would you focus effort on a prospect you know you are never going to sell?

Once there was a business owner who embraced the challenge of selling Sam's Wholesale Club. He knew he was never going to sell Sam's - his product was not a brand name, appealed to a small niche. But he went to work on the opportunity anyway, without hope, yet with a method to his madness.

He secured an appointment to present his line, and then developed 4 new lines of product for Sam's. Two of them made it to the planogram room. Predictably, neither was accepted.

But now, he had 4 lines of new product to offer his "regular customers." His regular customers could prevent his going from good to great. They would buy his existing line, and thus, weren't a sufficient motivation to develop new ideas.

Sam's Wholesale Club provided sufficient motivation for new ideation. And his regular customers were the beneficiaries of this effort.

To stimulate non-stop innovation, always keep on hand at least one impossible dream prospect - the prospect you know you are never going to sell.

Related to the impossible dream prospect is the 3 Pipe approach - a sustained focus on a problem. The metaphor is drawn from the Sherlock Holmes story, "The Man with the Twisted Lip." In solving the problem, Holmes remarks, "It was a 3-pipe problem."

It means he applied a sustained focus on the problem.

How often have you provided a sustained focus on a critical problem or opportunity for 1 hour, 3 hours, 8 hours straight?

In his book <u>Thinking Fast and Slow,</u> Kahneman distinguishes between two types of thinking - System 1 (intuitive) and System 2 (thoughtful). It's delightful to operate intuitively, in the moment, with System 1 thinking.

The problems are our intuition:

1) Can be wrong.
2) Isn't generally exhaustive in identifying and evaluating options.

System 2 - the 3 Pipe problem - provides the exhaustive analysis.

Once a business owner was facing ruin, over the proposed non-renewal of a contract. The customer didn't object to the business owner's performance, only to the business size - it was too small. Big companies like to do business with big companies.

Applying the "do or die" principle to thinking, the owner spent 8 hours straight identifying and thinking through all the options. He kept testing them in his mind till he found one that seemed relative bullet proof.

The next day he implemented the idea and succeeded.

Is there any challenge important enough in your life right now to merit a 3 Pipe approach, on a Do or Die basis?

You are one step closer to emotional intoxication.

CHAPTER 9
BOLD VISION, BOLD BEHAVIOR

If you aren't achieving what you want, ask yourself if you are bold enough in your vision and behavior. We have already explored social selling (be my friend) vs. business selling (allow me to earn the right to your business). It takes bold behavior to transform from social selling to business selling.

A related idea is are you being sufficiently unconventional?

George Bernard Shaw wrote:

"The reasonable man adapts himself to the world; the unreasonable one persists in trying to adapt the world to himself. Therefore, all progress depends on the unreasonable man."

In the previous chapters, we discussed several cases driven by "bold vision, and bold behavior." In the problem of the early class, we found:

1) Bold vision: sleeping late (for the student); saving the class from being dropped (for the university).

2) Bold behavior: challenging the existing order - seeking your own path as opposed to doing what you are told. In Shaw's language "being unreasonable."

In the case of the CPA's we found:

1) Bold vision: showing the CPAs how to substantially increase their closing ratio

2) Bold behavior: pushing forward with no experience or product offering, let alone industry specific experience.

What, if anything, is holding you back from conceiving and boldly implementing a bold vision? Pause for a moment; think about a tough, but meaningful opportunity you are pursuing. What unconventional behavior - bold vision, bold behavior - can you apply?

In the "do or die" packaging case cited above, we found:

1) Bold vision: showing the industry a new, customized way to develop packaging.

2) Bold behavior: going around the manufacturer to the end user.

Is anything causing you to hesitate? We all have innovative ideas.

As a salesperson, you have these strategic resources to help frame your bold vision, bold behavior: the existing offer, the future offer in development, your sample shop, your customer base, references from existing customers, your personal relationships and credibility.

Sometimes fear of failure chokes us, and we hesitate in moving forward. Perhaps it makes sense for you to try your idea in low risk situations.

Here's an example of bold behavior in a high-risk situation, which developed a powerful innovative selling method.

The seller needed to close a consulting sale; there were urgent bills to pay. Right now! Talk about a sense of urgency. It took one year to secure a 1st meeting with the prospect, a three-hour cross-examination by the leadership of the 5 operating companies. Invited back the next day by the division leader with whom he would work, the seller had another successful three-hour meeting. That evening, the entrepreneur/owner emailed the seller, requesting a proposal.

The seller was concerned the owner would say, "Your price is too high." You have probably had that experience, what would you do?

This seller asked the owner to check references, before providing a quote.

The owner wrote back saying he would check references after receiving the proposal, if still interested. What would you do at this point? It's your sales call.

The seller went "all in", writing back the reference check was an essential part of the proposal. How else could the owner know the seller's work ethic, creativity, and ability to collaborate and be flexible? If the owner had a sense of urgency in the future, "check my references and I will prepare a proposal." The owner started checking references within 15 minutes. The seller reports that he dies a small death each time he goes "all in" with a high-stakes situation. He also reports he has a great sense of integrity and self-respect.

For a video, see: http://bit.ly/texashold-em

Here's another bold move, which is often necessary and can become an "all in" scenario - helping the king or queen off the throne:

What might make it Worse.......

Many owners are accustomed to being the king or queen

URGENCY BASED SELLING®

BOMBADIL

In order to help many decision-makers, we need to move them from closed mindset to open mindset. They need to become vulnerable and open to change. When an owner is accustomed to being the "king of the castle" for 10, 20, 30 years, it can be a very bold move to help them off the throne, to consider options. Sometimes, we need to state the issue explicitly and name the elephant in the room.

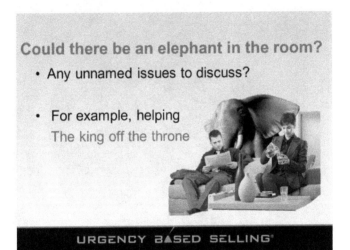

It's probably a good idea to get permission to do so, ask for a green light to speak openly. Consider this: when an owner knows you will speak your mind when trying to earn the right to business, when common sense says, "don't offend," they may just begin to accept you as a trusted advisor.

Helping the "king off the throne is disruptive," it disrupts the social norms, the expected behavior. Are you being disruptive enough to achieve your goals?

A salesman gave a strong example of disruptive bold behavior, when cold calling on a prospect that refused to see him. The prospect wouldn't respond to phone calls, emails, or snail mail. Nothing. The salesman sent a note saying he would be stopping by the following Monday. He told the guard at the security station he was here to see the buyer - and got through. He told the receptionist she was here to see the buyer - and waited 45 minutes till the buyer came down to the lobby.

"Thanks for inviting me to visit." Said the salesperson

"What are you doing here, we don't have an appointment." Said the buyer.

"I'm here to solve your production problems."

"But I don't have any production problems."

They two repeated these two lines, until finally the buyer looked at the salesperson's messaging and agreed to test the product. Bold, disruptive behavior.

A key challenge for salespeople is "earning the right" to meeting with C-Suite executives. Here are some ideas to consider:

1) **Type 3 knowledge**

There are 3 types of knowledge:

a) Type 1 - what we know

b) Type 2 - what we know we don't know

c) Type 3 - what we don't realize we don't know

Farsighted CEO's should want to learn about relevant Type 3 knowledge - offering an education on what they don't realize they don't know. Telling the prospect, you are offering Type 3 knowledge, can be a strong pattern interrupter, prompting the prospect to continue the conversation by asking, "What is type 3 knowledge?" You need to be prepared to back up your statement with a compelling bold vision.

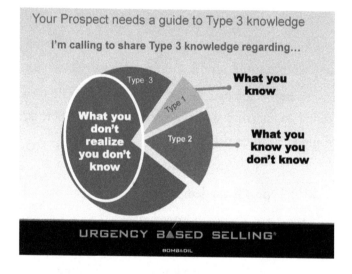

2) **The economic justification**

The Ben Franklin method compares pros to cons in helping a prospect make any decision - including whether to grant us an audience. We usually need to monetize the advantages we bring with an economic justification or an ROI.

3) Improving company culture

CEO's should welcome ideas for improving company culture and alignment. What do you have to offer?

What happens when your offer doesn't convey enough value to the CEO to merit his/her time? How do you transform your offer of small gains into a "bold vision?"

Perhaps no one has noticed this idea, which is: adopting your solution conveys to the organization pennies and nickels count. When everyone knows we pay attention to pennies and nickels, we are often more attentive to big decisions. And thereby, consequently, saving the organization big dollars.

In fact, your offer may become an indicator KPI to an organization - confirming organizational health.

Note: If we have learning mindset, we know some failure is inevitable; it's part of the learning process. When we innovate, we are learning about something, which probably doesn't exist yet. We are beginning a conversation with the future.

In the book <u>Innovating</u>, author Luis Perez-Breva, reminds us innovating is built on experimentation and failure. The sooner we start experimenting at scale, with the resources we have today, the sooner we begin eliminating failures and crafting a successful road forward.

The author has been evolving a selling method - Urgency Based Selling - for 23 years. This means forming hypotheses and making many mistakes for 23 years. There were core principles at the outset - including "do or die" and "bold vision, bold behavior." Most of the rest was developed from responding to client's needs, learning from clients' best practices, and trying out new ideas.

In **Middle Class Millionaire**, the authors point out a core success trait for those who rise from middle class to millionaire is working on the problem over time, learning from failure. This process leads to continuous improvement, often solidifying a defendable position.

You are one step closer to emotional intoxication.

CHAPTER 10
INNOVATING TO SCALE - USING WHAT WE HAVE

In his book **Innovating**, author Luis Perez-Breva, encourages us to innovate to scale, using the materials, methods and contacts we have.

"How did you do that?"

Wouldn't it be great if you could stimulate this admiring response from a prospect? This could be an essential part of your strategy to become known as the "idea person." This is a great personal brand - the idea person - something you can generally do with the materials at hand, working at current scale.

This chapter offers a research idea, which should provoke this response - and a way to get introductions.

Our existing business model - including our resources, relationships, customers, prospects, strategy, culture, vendors, company team members, competition - is a prototype for our future business. We should always ask ourselves this question:

"What do we need, what can we add, to scale up with impact to the next level?"

Each salesperson should ask this question regarding his/her book of business.

It's easy to say that **we need more** advertising, inventory, product variety; we need lower prices and longer dating terms.

These proposed changes place the locus of control elsewhere. In effect, no improvement is possible until external changes are made.

Is there nothing we can do, to scale up with what we have? Sell more of what we have with innovative sales behavior?

We have explored several approaches for innovative selling to scale up sales, including:

1) A "Do or Die" mindset

2) The learning mindset

3) Bold vision, bold behavior

4) Non-conventional behavior

These approaches are under our control. They are gateways to an innovative mindset.

What specifically can we do to:

1) Earn the right to more 1st appointments.

2) Resuscitate an opportunity which has gone "radio silent."

3) Close more business now?

This chapter focuses on two ideas - research and introductions - to help you scale up sales.

Research

Are you employing easy to use - often free of charge research tools - available to us on the internet?

For instance, a great way to positively attract a prospect's attention is with the website upgrade comparison. This allows you to say, "From your website upgrades, you obviously care how you look. I am reaching out to you to help you look better in… {your specialty}.

Here's how the Urgency Based Selling website looked in March 2016:

Bomb△dil
Breakthrough Selling

About Bombadil   Testimonials   References   Contact

Welcome to **Bombadil** where you'll find a revolutionary approach to the selling process. We can show you how to break through the barriers, and rethink how you organize and manage the sales organization for maximum effectiveness.

Services: The Selling Process

Creating Urgency (Avoiding Interest) ▶

Cannon Fodder Evaluation ▶

Moxie Test Training ▶

Blackmail Elimination ▶

Masterful Presentations ▶

▲ Take the Bombadil
Assessment Survey for
a **FREE** evaluation

Services: Management

Sales Training ▶

Sales Management ▶

Organizational Effectiveness ▶

Annual Sales Audits ▶

Sales Audits for Acquisitions ▶

Recruiting, the Missing Link ▶

News & Events

The Art of the Deal
Accounting Today Article

Bombadil Seminar Series

▲ Sign up for the Bombadil
e-newsletter

Testimonials

'The proof is in the pudding; initial observations suggest participants are enjoying a 20-30% increase in sales. They are doing new sales behaviors and

What do Frank Lloyd Wright's innovative

Bomb△dil
Key Selling Concepts

▲ Material Difference

▲ Proof Criteria

▲ Closing Conditions

▲ Moxie

Here's how it looks today:

To make this comparison, use the Wayback machine, found at this URL:

https://web.archive.org/

The Wayback machine saves websites, showing their histories.

Type in the URL of the company you want to research:

And select the month and year you want to view:

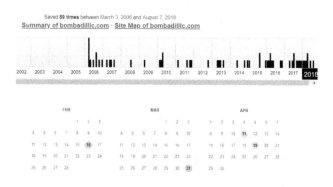

Does it make a difference? Could we just reach out and say, "You care about how you look"? Or "You care about best practices, continuous improvement."

When you show the website upgrade, you are "fishing with bait." You are putting skin in the game. Validating your statement with research. You are more credible. And, odds are, you will be more successful.

Another great tool to research small and medium sized businesses, typically not covered by the national news media, is **America's News**.

America's News is a database of regional newspapers. You can usually access it for free through your local library. It's one of many great research resources you can access online through your library. (First you need to secure a library card, and then visit the reference desk for get on line access.)

Here's a URL for America's news, which I can access through my library:

http://bit.ly/americas-news

A final research method, often overlooked, is to demonstrate core value alignment. Most websites present the company core values, either directly or indirectly. By copying the core values from both your prospect's website and your own website, you can demonstrate core value alignment.

These are three door openers based on your research.

Introductions

Your greatest selling asset is usually your existing delighted customers. They should produce a high Net Promoter Score, as described in **<u>The Ultimate Question</u>**.

Are you appropriately tapping this network?

How can you improve your lead flow through introductions?

First, do your research.

Make a list of your 10-20 biggest fans. Next, make sure you are LinkedIn with them. Finally, look at their LinkedIn connections and see whom you would like to meet.

Wait for the Magic Moment of Access.

The magic moment is when the customer makes a request which you satisfy. You confirm the customer is delighted, that there are no further needs. Now is a great time to ask for an introduction. You have access and the clients are delighted.

Research and introductions are two great ways to develop new opportunities.

What do these methods suggest to you? What else can you do to generate more first appointments?

You are one step closer to emotional intoxication.

CHAPTER 11
THE PRE-MORTEM FOR CONFIRMATION BIAS

Video link: http://bit.ly/confirm-bias

We all like to be right, and often focus on the data, which confirms either preconceived notions or the outcome we seek - e.g. the customer will buy, or we have a great new idea.

As Kahneman observes in <u>Thinking Fast and Slow</u>, when our subconscious presents a new idea to us, we can't tell if it's a good idea or a poor idea – till we validate it.

A salesman returns from a sales call jubilant. When asked why he was so happy, he responded: "The call was a slam dunk, I crushed it."

Everyone is happy to hear it. "What makes you say so?" Asks his boss.

"They loved me."

Unfortunately, the prospect never took another call from the salesperson. He was being positive just to get the salesperson out of his office. The salesperson suffered from confirmation bias. We need to consider what went wrong, and how do we prevent a repeat?

In general, if it's easy, low risk and low cost to validate, we just go ahead and try an idea. What if it's expensive, time consuming and/or risky?

How can we arm ourselves to avoid confirmation bias?

Professor Tetlock at Wharton has a panel of super forecasters who have substantially above average ability to forecast the future. In his book **Superforecasters,** he describes the methods they use.

Video link: http://bit.ly/battleplan1

One key technique is the Pre-Mortem. It's projecting what a Post-Mortem might look like, to prevent the need for a Post-Mortem.

You ask yourself a question, "Why am I going to lose this sale, for sure?" Even when you are sure you will close it.

Another framing, for any decision, is "Why is this the worst decision I ever made?"

Once you develop a legitimate answer, you go to work developing a counter-strategy.

Here's an example from sales:

Joe is a software solutions salesperson. He has several opportunities in the pipeline, but hasn't closed anything. Top management is getting impatient.

Then, Joe has a breakthrough to report. He is the sole bidder for a large requirement at a Fortune 100 company, which should close in a month or two. Everyone is ecstatic.

However, as time passes, the start date keeps getting pushed back. And management begins to wonder if there really is an opportunity. They do a pre-mortem.

VP Sales: Joe, let's do a Pre-mortem. Tell me why you don't have a chance of closing this sale?

Joe: There is no problem, it's in the bag.

VP Sales: I know, but this is a mindset shift for brainstorming purposes. It's pretend.

Joe: But it's a done deal.

VP Sales: I know, but let's do the exercise.

Joe: Well, maybe our price is too high.

VP Sales: Any evidence of this?

Joe: No

VP Sales: Let's try another reason.

Joe: But the order is mine, not a problem.

VP Sales: Just try.

Joe: Well, my contact's boss's boss (2 levels up) just changed.

VP Sales: Do you know him?

Joe: No

VP Sales: Could the new boss affect this decision?

Joe: Maybe

VP Sales: Let's try to get to know him.

The VP Sales pushed Joe to get something in writing, regarding a commitment from the big customer. Here's what the decision-maker put in writing:

Hi Joe,

We will be going out to bid in the next month and you will be included on the bidder's list.

Quite a bit difference from "it's in the bag."

Joe was fired.

Another team member pursued the opportunity, he didn't close it, and they never had a chance.

Has this ever happened to you: you thought it was a slam-dunk and you never had a chance?

PIK's - payments in kind - a very special antidote to pre-mortems, can help; it's the subject of the next chapter.

Note: Here's a variation on the pre-mortem used by the author to create Urgency Based Selling - If everything I have done doesn't work, what's my next move.

You are one step closer to emotional intoxication.

CHAPTER 12
THE PAYMENT IN KIND
METHOD (PIK'S)

Watch what people **do**, not what they **say.**

Watching what prospects do can lead to a revolutionary innovation in your selling.

Two salespeople returned to the office late one afternoon. They were both exuberant, both sure they were about to close a big customer deal. You judge which meeting was stronger, based on how the two salespeople answer this question from the VP Sales, "What makes you so sure?"

Salesperson 1 answered, "They loved me."

Salesperson 2 answered, "They filled out a credit application."

There are two kinds of sales meetings – safe and serious. In a safe meeting, the prospect is safe, because she will never give you a stick of business. She's in the meeting for a different reason than you – probably a price check, or a free education, maybe a free lunch. But one thing's for sure; you will never get any business. <u>Video:</u> http://bit.ly/3Fatalflaws

In a serious conversation, the prospect has an urgent need and is willing to discuss it with you. Serious doesn't mean you close, it means you opened.

How can you tell the difference between safe and serious? Wouldn't it be fantastic if there was a high probability method to determine if it's wheat or chaff, a qualified opportunity or a waste of time?

Watch the **<u>Payments in Kind</u>**, it's a great way to qualify an opportunity, and an important area for sales innovation.

A payment in kind is evidence the prospect is serious. It's what he/she does to show it's a real opportunity, not a price check. Selling is a contact sport, not a spectator sport. PIK's are how the prospect makes contact.

PIK's can be:

1) Reference checks.

2) Introductions to a team member or a direct report

3) Visiting our facility.

4) Filling out a 3-question survey before the first meeting.

5) Completing a credit application.

In the last chapter, Joe sure could have used a strong PIK. The commitment to be invited to bid was a weak PIK, which he only obtained when pushed to do so by his VP Sales.

In an earlier chapter, we discussed a seller who wouldn't quote until the prospect checked his references – first. This was a very strong PIK - a showing of interest by the prospect. In Texas Hold'em terms, it's a tell.

PIK's help solve the fundamental paradox in selling. For every two-three steps you take forward, you often take one backwards.

When the prospect invites you to visit or act, you want to do so with a sense of urgency. Otherwise, if you act like you don't care, why should the prospect care?

However, when you do act with urgency, the prospect often takes this as neediness, wonders if he can get a fire sale, steal it.

When you sell with PIK's from the outset, you teach the prospect you will be strong – from the outset. You are conditioning the prospect to diminish or pre-empt economic negotiating, by negotiating strongly from the beginning.

You have probably heard the saying, "pay me now or pay me later."

You will probably have to negotiate at some time. Better to negotiate strongly from the outset over non-economic issues. Negotiate over reasonable behavior – PIK's.

Selling with PIKs causes the prospect to show she is serious; it's like a tell in poker.

The most important part of your follow-up email, after a sales call, is the PIK. It's what the prospect agreed to do.

Salespeople usually appreciate PIK's, as they show the prospect respects them.

PIK's can become an important part of price negotiations. If you find you must reduce your economic price, get a PIK in trade – perhaps 2-3 introductions. It's a bad idea to reduce your price without a quid pro quo – it makes the prospect wonder, "how low is low?"

A final note on PIK's - earlier we identified the paradox of urgency vs. neediness. When the salesperson shows a sense of urgency, does he/she also convey neediness? To prevent or lessen this likelihood, sell strongly with PIK's. From the outset, expect the prospect to act reasonably, to do the behaviors a serious prospect should do. By insisting on reasonable behavior from the outset, we are beginning the bargaining for price, without price ever being mentioned. By the time we get to price, the likelihood is much greater the prospect will accept our price as reasonable.

You are one step closer to emotional intoxication.

CHAPTER 13
RISK AVERSION

Video link: http://bit.ly/less-risky

Once there was a consultant who had never worked in prospect's industry. He provided 10 references who furnished a clean bill of health. Yet, the prospect said,

"I know this works in all the other businesses you helped. But my business is different." Is it?

The prospect has risk aversion and is avoiding risk. Here's a test to help you evaluate your own sense of risk aversion. What would you rather have?

1) $5,000 sure thing, or

2) We flip a coin; heads you get $10,000, tails you get nothing?

If you are like most people, you would prefer the sure thing, the $5,000.

What happens if we reduce the sure thing to $4,000 or we flip a coin, where you get $10,000 or nothing? What about $3,000 vs. the coin toss?

Based on Kahneman's work on risk aversion - described in his book **<u>Thinking Fast and Slow</u>** - the average person would accept as little as $2,500 sure thing, to avoid the coin toss. Video link: http://bit.ly/less-risky

We are, by nature, risk averse - we don't like risk. Our reptilian brain is programmed for flight or flight in the face of risk.

We like the sure bet, but innovation requires we step out into the unknown and take chances.

On the other hand, if we want a prospect to buy/try our product, we need to assuage their sense of risk, reduce their perceived sense of risk.

Risk aversion is a major reason prospects avoid our offer. They see the incumbent solution as the sure thing, our offer as the "coin toss."

Testimonials can be helpful, particularly if the prospect knows the person providing the testimonial. If you are on a level playing field, and only you provide testimonials, you probably have the edge - everything else being held equal.

If the prospect is relatively happy with the incumbent, you need to address the perceived risk, or the prospect will want a discount - sometimes a deep discount - to address the perceived risk.

Testimonials - in isolation - can be rejected as anecdotal. The way to supercharge testimonials is to link them to your processes.

Here's a four-step process for addressing risk aversion:

1) Our strong processes (which you demonstrate),

2) Deliver consistent reliable statistics

3) Which allows us to provide a guarantee

4) Which is validated by testimonials

Where you have SOP's - standard operating procedures - you can do the SOP test. Show your prospect the table of contents of your SOP's - invite them to visit your facility, select any 2-3 at random and verify you adhere to them.

Alternatively, you can focus your marketing on identifying and selling risk takers.

These are the first people who will try your new product.

In retail, you might find a "path of innovation," a group of retailers who consistently try new products, before they become mainstream.

Every business should identify a "path of innovation" to get early trial and acceptance for its products.

You are one step closer to emotional intoxication.

CHAPTER 14
DO ROOT CAUSE
ANALYSIS AND THE STANDARD
SALES CALL

Video link: http://bit.ly/root-cause1

Do you know the root cause of any problem you face?

A traveler looked forward to driving his car, upon landing at his nearby airport. It was a measure of being back in control. Imagine his disappointment when the car wouldn't start. AAA investigated the problem and said, "You need a new battery." So, the traveler bought a new battery.

But it didn't seem reasonable. It was a new car; the battery shouldn't have failed. So…

The next day, he took the car back to the dealership. The service writer advised him,

"You probably left your door open, or the headlights on."

But it didn't seem reasonable. So, he spoke to the service manager who said,

"We have been having this problem lately, it's the electronic control module causing the battery to discharge." And they reprogrammed the module, fixing the problem.

By focusing on the surface problem, the battery, this motorist would have replaced one battery after another, accumulating a battery collection. This wasn't the root cause.

How about applying the root cause approach to your selling? If you aren't satisfied with your results, what is the root cause?

1) Lousy prospects - not getting the Glengarry leads.

2) Poor offer - pricing, product, inventory, dating isn't right.

Yet, others may be selling successfully with the same context.

It's a good idea to test your standard sales call, your step by step process for initiating an opportunity, warming up a prospect, learning their needs, designing and presenting a solution and getting agreement to move forward. http://bit.ly/Standard-sales

Once you have a standard sale call, you can begin to experiment, comparing your practice to a known standard and trying new ideas.

A standard sales call will help you show the prospect you are:

1) A serious professional (research and advanced agenda).

2) Courteous, engaging - techniques for warming up the prospect.

3) Mindful, a good diagnostician - based on your fact finding.

4) A Problem solver based on your proposed solution.

5) Someone who gets the job done.

Let's review some techniques you use from the standard sales call:

1) Research - core value alignment

It is usually relatively easy to discover a prospect's core values from their website or other research online. When you know their core values, and they align with yours, this sets up an easy way to find common ground. Here's a script you can use:

"I noticed you emphasize the following core values on your website (bring a print out). How did your company select these values? I was encouraged to see these values for they align with our values (show a printout of your company's core values).

I don't know if we have a fit yet, because you haven't shared your needs. But I do know this... companies that have the same core values usually like to do business together."

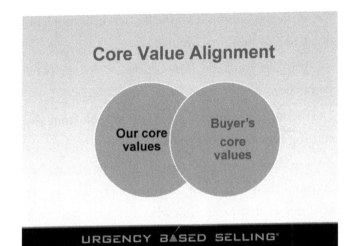

2) The prospect's background - the bookend approach

We can often learn a lot about the prospect from online research, particularly the Linked In profile. To learn the whole story, the bookend approach can be helpful:

"Tell me a little about your background. Were you always the ..current position…at your company? No. How did you start out, what was the journey like over time…?"

With this approach you will often hear much of a prospect's professional life story.

You can conclude this section by saying, (when you believe it to be true),

"Wow, that's quite a journey you took from your starting point to where you are now.

I'm sure you are proud of what you have accomplished and want to protect it. We are very sensitive to first protecting what you have built, then offering you options to make it even better."

3) The prospect's motivation

If you have properly warmed up a prospect with research, professionalism, and customization, they might be ready to share the following:

a) Why they agreed to see you?

b) Why now (why not 6 months ago) - this is often the money question.

c) Their vision for the future - how it will be when you fix the problem?

4) **Addressing risk aversion**

The bookend technique sets up discovering risk aversion. Here's a script you can use,

"A little while ago, we discussed how you want to protect what you have built. How do you do this when evaluating a new vendor like us? How do you address the risk?"

5) **The buyer's remorse approach**

When you have a verbal agreement from a prospect, but not a written confirmation, it's a great time to apply the buyer's remorse approach.

Here's what you say,

"Thanks for selecting our offer. We are thrilled to have you as a new client. Our marketing department has asked us to find out something for them. Customers select us for many different reasons. Could you advise the top 3 reasons you chose us?"

This is a very important question. If the prospect doesn't have a good answer to the question, they may not understand the decision. It would fall apart the first time someone challenges them on it.

If the prospect doesn't have a good reason for selecting your offer, you still have plenty of selling to do.

You are one step closer to emotional intoxication.

CHAPTER 15
HOW DO YOU IMPROVE A SALES ORGANIZATION CONTINUOUSLY?

One approach is to generate a constant flow of new ideas and implement them. Here are some ideas you might consider implementing:

1) The Book Club Approach

The sales leader selects a book, which everyone reads. You get together once a week for a short period of time to discuss a chapter.

Where there is a need for cultural alignment, this could be the book's focus.

2) The Sales Huddle

Periodically meet to discuss specific challenges and opportunities; this presents another chance to teach and to learn.

You might schedule a daily or weekly meeting where all team members offer a case history - e.g. on handling the objection: "Your price is too high."

Team members would demonstrate how they convinced the prospect to focus on total cost in sue vs. first cost.

3) Selling Tools

When you face a problem, it is desirable to develop a worksheet - for economic justification, an excel spreadsheet - which helps team members prove their case.

For longer-term projects, you want a battle plan. Here's an example:

Video link: bit.ly/battleplan1

4) Encouraging new ideas - promote the "idea factory"

Encourage team members to disagree - constructive disagreement is a good thing.

(For example, The Five Dysfunctions of teams.)

5) Ideally, everyone develops problem solving skills

It's a good practice to encourage team members to solve their own problems. Before they approach leadership for help, they should complete a brief form with these categories:

a) What is the problem?

b) What options are you considering?

c) What do you recommend and why?

d) What cost is there, if any?

6) When team members are stumped, encourage them

I know you don't know the answer, but if you did, how might it look?

7) To develop younger team members, learn from the Polynesians

In ancient Polynesian society, younger people were asked to "adopt a tree", oversee its growth and ultimately build a canoe from it.

150 years ago, being 20 years old was middle aged. Younger team members are capable of great results if given the opportunity.

What lower risk opportunity can you offer a sales team member, to help them develop risk taking and thinking skills?

8) What did you learn from mistakes?

As long as a risk isn't taken recklessly, it's OK to try to new ideas and learn from mistakes.

A key question - perhaps in a huddle - might be: what risks did you take this week, what mistakes did you make, what did you learn?

You are one step closer to emotional intoxication.

CHAPTER 16
THE YIN AND YANG OF SELLING - A PAUSE BEFORE EMOTIONAL INTOXICATION

Most of the ideas in this book are about doing - doing something you haven't done or doing it more intensely and completely (yang). This chapter is more focused on not doing, the yin of selling. And the importance of oscillating between the states of yin and yang - between doing and not-doing.

When opening new customers in the face of resistance, you typically need yang - a strong positive case, bold vision, and bold behavior.

When you make a breakthrough, you need to switch to yin - the listening mode.

There is usually only enough oxygen in the room for one person to talk at a time. If we talk, we consume the talking "oxygen" and the prospect doesn't talk. We fail to learn the closing conditions - the series of conditions which, when met, result in the sale.

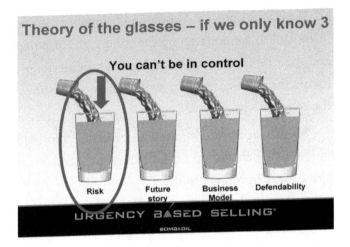

The theory of the glasses tells us there are two steps to proving our case - first discovering the decision criteria (the glasses), then showing we satisfy the criteria (filling the glasses). See video: http://bit.ly/theory_glasses

In the above illustration, the prospect told us their key decision criteria were:

1) Meeting their risk needs.

2) The bold vision of what we can do.

3) The value of this vision.

4) The time frame in which it can be accomplished.

If we don't know the closing conditions, we can't be in control. If we don't set up the context for listening and then listen very well - asking appropriate follow up questions - we won't know the closing conditions, the prospect's must-haves.

So we need yin - we need to oscillate from bold vision, bold behavior to a more passive state and create space for the prospect to talk.

A yin mindset based on gratitude also facilitates integrating the sales function into the corporate culture - with the ethos of the humble warrior.

Sometimes, successful salespeople are toxic to the organization and lack gratitude. They hold themselves above others.

Gratitude for opportunity is the glue, which connects salespeople to the team, and stabilizes them internally.

Gratitude for opportunity also attracts prospects.

The mindset of the humble warrior - grateful for opportunity - binds the salesperson to customers and the organization. For the video, see http://bit.ly/humble-warrior1 .

There is another important reason we need yin - to prepare for emotional intoxication. If we are in the "do or die" hero mode all the time, we are likely to burn out. The yin state is the balance, the grounding, the recovery, the relaxation, and the renewal state. It stabilizes emotional intoxication.

The cyclical, daily activities of life provide yin. To achieve heightened mindfulness here are two practices which bring a yin state of mind: meditation and yoga.

What are your practices to balance yang with yin?

And prepare you for sustainable emotional intoxication?

CHAPTER 17
A PATH TO EMOTIONAL INTOXICATION AND INNOVATION - A 2 WAY STREET

Nietzsche hinted at the method in <u>Twilight of the Idols</u>:

"The essential thing about intoxication is the feeling of increased power and plentitude."

(Page 47).

Nietzsche, Friedrich, 1998. <u>Twilight of the Idols</u>, United Kingdom: Oxford University Press, translated by Duncan Large

A Formula for emotional intoxication

Moral Certainty

\+

Meditative State

\+

Heroic Mindset

=

Emotional Intoxication

URGENCY BASED SELLING®

BOMBADIL

Emotional intoxication has this revolutionary quality – as both means and ends. As an end, it can be the ultimate, positive psychological state. As means, it provides the fuel to be self-renewing and generates creative output in productive work (including selling). In effect, emotional intoxication makes this possible: perpetual selling innovation and success. Here are the key elements:

a) The heroic feeling

b) Moral certainty, balance by

c) The meditative state

We must achieve threshold levels of each to sustain emotional intoxication.

First and foremost, one must live a heroic existence. This requires a commitment to creativity, to search and discovery, combined with competence and risk taking. We have discussed these qualities throughout the book with chapters on:

1) Do or Die

2) Learning Mindset

3) Bold Vision, Bold Behavior

4) Innovating to Scale

5) Overcoming Self-Limiting Assumptions

All these ideas are both ends in themselves - valuable thinking tools - at the same time they contribute to achieving heroic behavior. When these activities produce enough heroic accomplishment, they generate an enduring <u>heroic feeling,</u> essential to emotional intoxication.

Living the heroic life doesn't suffice for emotional intoxication. We need moral certainty; a guilt-free existence, is an essential underpinning to generating stable emotional intoxication. Without moral certainty, we would have contempt for what we do. Threshold levels of the "heroic feeling" and moral certainty must be achieved to attain emotional intoxication.

This is an important reason to discover and advocate the "bold vision," to discover and provide Type 3 knowledge.

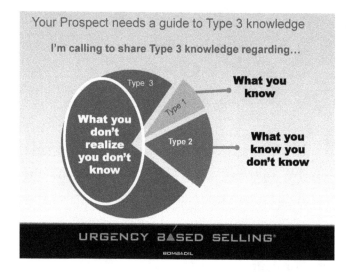

To save the drowning prospect who tells you, "I'm good." They are on a false summit, we can help them to a higher summit of well-being.

You can only sustain these activities in the long term with a sense of moral certainty - that you are doing the right thing.

All of this mental content must be mediated by the use of reason.

How does this work? Following Francis Bacon's admonition to "identify the intermediaries," consider how emotional intoxication impacts creativity – the cause and affect mechanism.

Studies correlate periods of robust creativity with non-linear, non-ordinary consciousness (e.g. drug induced). How might this be true? The answer lies in the relationship between the "rational grid" and creativity. The rational grid is our continuous rational effort to integrate all mental content and sensory input. Fundamentally, we face an either-or choice – the rational grid or creativity; rational grid suspension liberates creativity.

Suspending the rational grid is possible and efficacious, providing raw material for creativity. A total rational grid suspension is contradictory, a <u>selective focus</u>, unencumbered by the normal internal dialogue - the continuous conversation we have with ourselves – is productive. The internal dialogue, in support of the rational grid, distracts us from non-linear, creative thought.

The selective focus evokes Casteneda's distinction between the tonal (the rational) and the nagual (the mystical). He asserts we need to suspend the internal dialogue to reach the mystical world. We have a similar need to oscillate between the rational grid and the creative state (with suspended internal dialogue) in an emotionally intoxicated state.

What emotional intoxication does is: help suspend the rational grid, which allows the creative flow to intensify. It permits a selective creative focus to emerge.

How, then, does one engage or re-engage the rational grid? The level or intensity of emotional intoxication fluctuates from a base level – consider starter cells for antibodies - to a threshold level, where the grid is suspended for a selective creative focus. The intensity of emotional intoxication is controlled through a variety of techniques, including meditation.

The fuel to start the non-stop creative process is the method of emotional intoxication. Once initiated, it is self-sustaining by the individual, at least for some duration.

Is it self-sustaining on a perpetual basis? Can we experience non-stop emotional intoxication?

Nietzsche condemns:

"The profound Greek who was in danger of craving a Buddhist denial of the will" (NIETZSCHE 1956, 60).

What if, instead of a thinking dichotomy, we embrace non-linear thinking, which includes non-conventional thought? Non-linear thought would have at least 3 components:

1) The meditative state.

2) The creative, inductive state.

3) States of non-ordinary consciousness, including those induced through breathing and music, such as holotropic breathworks.

Testable creative hypotheses, which we later validate by logic, are often or perhaps predominantly generated by non-linear, non-conventional thought; emotional intoxication fuels these thoughts. Consider in this respect Polanyi's "imaginative outthrustings" - reaching out in non-conventional thoughts. In addition to generating creative output, these non-linear states generate emotional fuel. The meditative state recharges our emotional batteries. The importance of non-linear thinking may be why Bacon and Nietzsche rejected "sterile" Aristotelian thought; they grasped the importance of suspending the rational grid.

One final important distinction is between the general state of emotional intoxication and peak experiences. Peak experiences are not sustainable in the long term. The ability to achieve peak experiences more consistently is facilitated by emotional intoxication. For instance, maintaining a baseline level of emotional intoxication enables Dionysian Union in a romantic relationship.

In summary, sustainable rational, emotional intoxication is a function of:

1) The heroic feeling

2) Moral certainty

3) Meditative rejuvenation

CHAPTER 18
WHEN YOU HEAR "HOUSTON WE HAVE A PROBLEM" – THE APOLLO 13 APPROACH, CREATING YOUR OWN SOLUTIONS

When the astronauts on Apollo 13 reported, "Houston we have a problem," the outlook seemed hopeless. What was the response in ground control? They "worked the problem." If NASA brought back the 3 astronauts, under impossible conditions, what are you willing to accept as impossible?

Are you willing to work the problem?

Here is a recap of 7 sales accelerators you can use:

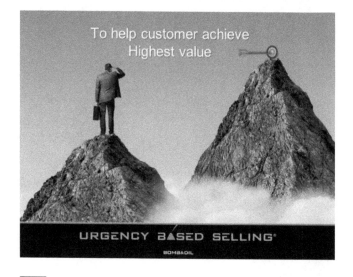

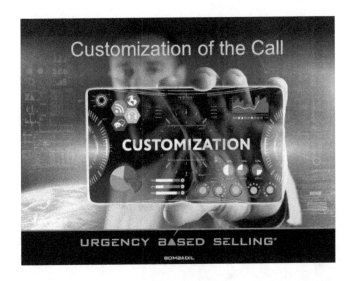

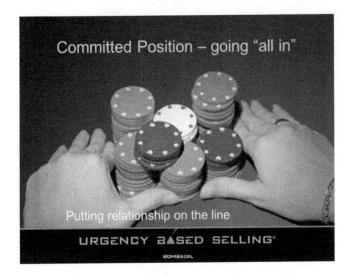

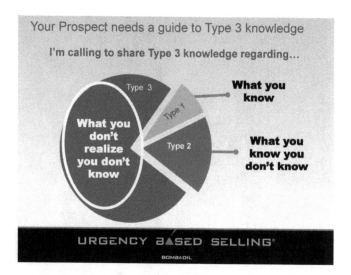

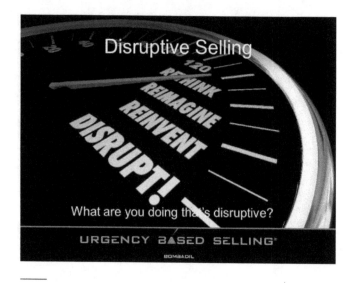

Still, there will be times when, even with all these accelerators, the "do or die" attitude and intense focus, you will still come up dry.

It might help to have some prompts – your own version of the **induction worksheet**.

This helps you create you new ideas when you need them.

To get your creative juices flowing, here are excerpts developed from Francis Bacon's <u>New Organon</u>, a study of the nature of heat.

The Privileged Instances for Induction – apply the questions to your problem.

Let's say the challenge is getting a meeting with a CEO.

Here are some thoughts from using the induction worksheet, a way to be thoughtful about securing a CEO Meeting:

Necessary meetings – CEO/top management only take necessary meetings.

What are the red flags – the forward-looking metrics the CEO/owner watches?

What causes a CEO to take a sales meeting? What is the tipping point?

Meetings are bundled with what qualities? They are bundled with problem solving, with coaching/interaction/culture. How can we offer these qualities?

Social meeting vs. business meeting – what makes them different? A business meeting has a schedule/agenda. It's linear. A social meeting is fun. Is there a way to make a business meeting fun?

Unique – anomalies in meetings – what makes a meeting time well spent:

1) breakthroughs without hiring;

2) 10x the cost of people attending;

3) level 10 meeting

4) unbelievable meetings.

These ideas can help us secure meetings with CEO's.

Here is the detailed thought process, with prompts, which led to these observations, based on the privileged instances in Bacon's book:

1st privileged instance are those that exhibit the nature under investigation in the subjects, which have nothing in common with other subjects but that very nature. It is evident that instances of this nature… are a quick route to confirming an exclusion." P. 136

The genus? White is the color common to many white things

Necessary meetings – CEO/top management only take necessary meetings.

2nd privileged instance – instances of transition p. 137

Bacon writes:

"These are instances in which the nature which we are looking for, if previously non-existent, is in transition to being, and if already existing, towards non-being." P. 137

"Instance of transition: let the nature to be sought be White or whiteness; an instance in transition to produce it is unbroken glass and powdered glass; also, plain water and water stirred to a foam."

"Instance of transition towards non-being of whiteness – melting snow." p. 138

What are the red flags – the forward-looking metrics the CEO/owner watches?

4th **privileged instance** – concealed instances

"As 4th of the privileged instances we put concealed instances, which we have also chosen to call instances of the twilight. They are almost opposite to revealing instances. For they exhibit the nature under investigation at its lowest strength, as if in its origins or earliest efforts, tentative and trying itself out, but concealed beneath a contrary nature and subdued by it."

{i.e. boundary conditions, editor's note}

Concealed instances give the best glimpse of themselves in small portions of substances. P. 141

Suppose the nature under investigation is attraction or the coming together of bodies. The most remarkable revealing instance of its form is the magnet. A concealed secret is a magnet armed with iron, or rather iron in an armed magnet.

What causes sales meetings? The tipping point?

5th privileged instance – Constitutive Instances – bundled instances

Bacon writes:

"Genuine forms are hidden in the depths and not easily discovered, and therefore, the thing itself and the feebleness of human understanding require that we should not neglect, but carefully observe particular forms, which group certain bundles of instances together in a common notion. For whatever unites a nature, however imperfectly, opens a way to the discovery of the forms."

Meetings are bundles with other qualities. These are important to CEOs: problem solving, coaching/interaction/culture.

6th privileged instance – Instances of Resemblance or Analogous Instances – parallels, physical similarities

"These are instances that reveal similarities and connections between things, not in the lesser forms (constitutive instances), but in the actual concrete object. Thus, they are like the first and lowest steps towards the unity of a nature. They do not establish any axiom directly from the beginning, but only point to some agreement between bodies.

Some instances of resemblance are the eye and a mirror; the structure of the ear and echoing places." p. 145

"Likewise the fins of fish and the feet of quadrupeds or the feet and wings of birds are resembling instances."

"These things aside, instances of resemblance should not be ignored in bigger matters, even in the actual configuration of the earth, such as Africa and the Peruvian region with the coastline extending to the Strait of Magellan. For both regions have similar isthmuses and similar promontories, and that does not happen without a reason." P. 147

Bacon writes:

"Similarly the mathematical postulate that "things equal to a third thing are equal to each other" corresponds with the structure of syllogism in logic, which joins things that agree in a middle term. Finally, it is very useful that as many people as possible should have a keen sense for tracing and tracking physical similarities and resemblances." P. 147

Social meeting vs. business meeting – schedule/ agenda/; party vs. linear meeting; vs. game = what makes it fun?

Productive?

7th privileged instance – unique instances, irregular

"These are instances, which reveal in concrete form bodies, which seem to be extraordinary and isolated in nature, having very little in common with other things of the same kind. The use of unique instances is like the use of concealed instances, to raise and unite nature for the purpose of discovering kinds or common natures, which are afterwards to be limited by means of genuine differentia." P. 147

"The inquiry should proceed until the properties and qualities found in things which can be regarded as wonders of nature are reduced and comprehended under some specific form or law... Whereas now, men's reasoning gets no further than to call these things secrets of nature or monstrosities, things without cause and exceptions to the general rule." P.148

"Examples are: sun and the moon among the stars; the magnet among stones; the elephant amongst quadrupeds, the sensation of sex among the kinds of touch; keenness of scent in dogs among kinds of smell." p. 148

"Such instances should be prized, because they sharpen and quicken inquiry, refreshing a mind staled by habit and by the usual course of things." P. 148

{Note: Kuhn's anomalies, editor's note}

Unique – anomalies in meetings – what makes a meeting time well spent:

1) breakthroughs without hiring;

2) 10x the cost of people attending;

3) level 10 meeting

4) unbelievable meetings.

These ideas can help us secure meetings with CEO's.

If you write to <u>andy@urgencybasedselling.net</u>, I will send you the entire induction worksheet.

CHAPTER 19
SUMMING UP

There is no end to our potential creativity. We looked at 16 different innovative methods, including:

a.   Take a Do or die approach.

b.   Beware Self-limiting assumptions.

c.   Develop your WOW toolbox.

d.   Change the Structure.

e.   Commit to a learning mindset.

f.   Embark on a life of bold vision, bold behavior.

g.   Innovate to scale - with the tools and resources you have.

h.   Use the pre-mortem, to anticipate crisis.

i.   The Payment in Kind principle, for qualification and commitment.

j.   Overcoming risk aversion.

k.   Commitment to discovering root causes.

l. Focusing on improving the sales organization continuously.

m. The Yin and Yang of Selling.

n. The Method of Emotional Intoxication.

o. Using an innovation worksheet, to develop new ideas whenever needed.

Let me know which ideas worked for you and what new approaches you developed. You can reach me at <u>andy@urgencybasedselling.net</u>

BIBLIOGRAPHY

Aristotle, 1963. **The Philosophy of Aristotle**, New York, NY: New American Library, translated by A.E. Wardman and J.L. Creed

Bacon, Francis. 2000 **The New Organon**, New York, NY: Cambridge University Press

Brown, Shona and Eisenhardt, Kathleen, 1998 **Competing at the Edge**, Harvard Business Press

Castaneda, Carlos, 1972. **Journey to Ixthlan**. New York, NY: Washington Square Press

Campbell, Joseph. 1949 **The Hero with a Thousand Faces**. 1st edition, Bollingen Foundation, 2nd edition, Princeton University Press. 3rd edition, New World Library, 2008.

D'aveni, Richard and, Robert E. Gunther. 1994 **Hypercompetition** Free Press

Dweck, Carol S. 2006. **Mindset: the new psychology of success**. New York: Random House.

Kahneman, Daniel. 2011 **Thinking, Fast and Slow**. New York: Farrar, Straus and Giroux

Kuhn, Thomas, 1996**. The Structure of Scientific Revolutions**. Chicago, Ill: University Of Chicago Press; 3rd edition

Nietzsche, Friedrich, 1998. **Twilight of the Idols**, United Kingdom: Oxford University Press, translated by Duncan Large

Perez-Breva, Luis, PhD, 2017 **Innovating: A Doer's Manifesto**, *MIT Press*

Polanyi, Michael and Prosch, Harry, 1975. **Meaning.** Chicago, Ill: University of Chicago Press

Porter, Michael, 1985 **Competitive Strategy,** The Free Press

Tetlock, Phillip and Gardner, Dan, 2015 - ***Superforecasting: The Art and Science of Prediction***, Random House

Yu-Lan, Fung, 1948. **The Short History of Chinese Philosophy**, New York, NY: The Free Press

ABOUT THE AUTHOR
ANDY GOLE

Andy helps salespeople achieve the impossible by coaching them to the heroic mindset.

For over 25 years, he has worked with CEOs, owners and corporate leaders throughout the US, helping them achieve great sales performance, while accelerating their sales process. During his career, Andy has thoroughly researched virtually all the popular sales processes. All have their strengths, and their shortcomings. From years of testing and evaluation, he developed the Urgency Based Selling® system, a unique approach founded on philosophies which drive and accelerate human behavior.

Andy contributes original content regularly to Forbes.com and Training Industry, as well as other notable business publications.

He is also a frequent speaker on the topics of business development, sales management, and selling process. If you would like to find out more about Andy as a presenter, please visit: https://www.urgencybasedselling.net/solutions/seminars/

For more information please visit the website: www.urgencybasedselling.net, or check out this 90 second video on how Urgency Based Selling is different: http://bit.ly/How_UBS_Is_Different

Wishing you 'heroic' sales success! - Andy

THE PHILOSOPHER OF SALES

CPSIA information can be obtained
at www.ICGtesting.com
Printed in the USA
FFHW022328160819
54329495-60019FF